The Master's Plan
Lessons from MOSES

by Pastor Fred Kasule

SHABAR PUBLICATIONS
www.shabarpublications.com

Most Shabar Publications products are available at special quantity discounts for bulk purchase for sales promotions, fund-raising and educational needs. For details, write Shabar Publications at may-orga1126@gmail.com.

The Master's Plan: Lessons from MOSES
by Pastor Fred Kasule

Published by Shabar Publications
3833 N. Taylor Rd.
Palmhurst, Texas 78573
www.shabarpublications.com
mayorga1126@gmail.com

Unless otherwise noted, all Scripture quotations are from the Amplified Bible, published in 1965 by the Lockman Foundation and Zondervan.

Another translation used is New King James Version of the Bible. Copyright@1979, 1980, 1982 by Thomas Nelson, Inc., publishers. Used by permission.

ISBN 978-1-955433-26-6

Content

Foreword

Since God called man into His service, the Lord has always sought a specific response. The response is usually a basic yes or no answer. If any man or woman accepts the obedience of the voice of the Lord, the instructions will be practical and challenging; yet without faith and discipline, that servant will find it impossible to please God. As the Scripture educates those who would be God pleasers, **"But without faith it is impossible to please Him, for he who comes to God must believe that He is and that He is a rewarder of those who diligently seek Him."** (Hebrews 11:6)

To be a servant who speaks and teaches God's revelations, a man must walk in the revelatory realm of the Lord. I believe this author is one of them. Pastor Fred Kasule is one of the most God-possessed men I have had the privilege of meeting.

After spending time with God in the secret place, the Master rewarded my dear friend Pastor Fred Kasule with the notes of this manuscript. This book is from the Lord and worthy of all acceptance.

In revisiting the life of Moses, the Spirit of the Lord has breathed upon His servant a freshness to bring about this transformative book. Pastor Fred Kasule, as always, does a masterful work in extracting the honey of revelation from the Scriptures and presents the hungry servant of Jesus with relevant, present-day truths that, if practiced, will surely inspire and impact any generation.

From birth to Moses' calling, Pastor Fred Kasule has brought to the forefront practical and enriching principles that, if followed, will ensure success in any forum.

Suppose today you wonder how you will enter God's plan for your life and stay the course amidst adversity. Meditate upon the notes written in this book. In that case, it is a roadmap for that man or woman who carries deep within an unquenchable fire and a passion to live for Jesus like there will be no tomorrow!

David Mayorga, *Director*
Masterbuilder Ministries
McAllen, Texas

Introduction

What makes you glad or sad? What breaks or blesses your heart?

Regardless of location, condition, or background, it's time to rise and act. The rest of your life can bless your family and those around you for generations.

Have you ever wondered about God's plan for the rest of your life?

As a pastor, I am often asked how to know God's plan precisely and whether He has a specific plan for each person's life.

It can be hard to know which path to take in life. Many have prayed about which direction they should take but have yet to receive immediate clarity.

This leads us to the question, what is God's plan for me?

Judges 13:12 says, **"So Manoah asked him, "When your words are fulfilled, what is to be the rule that governs the boy's life and work?"**

A barren couple was promised a son, and the above scripture was Manoah's prayer to God before Samson was born.

What if, when we were born, we came with an instruction manual that God wrote for us?

A manual outlining where we should live, what schools to attend, what careers we should pursue, and what we should do to follow His plan for our lives.

Sometimes, it can be difficult to understand what God wants for us over the noise of the world and the sounds of all the obligations pulling at us. The truth is, God knows what He wants for any of us regardless of where we find ourselves today. He has the blueprint for our lives drawn up.

His plan for your life was designed before you were born. (Jeremiah 1:5-9, Psalm 139, Ephesians 2:10)

Chapter 1

Born at the Right Time!

"At that time, Moses was born." (Acts 7:20)

While reading and meditating upon the life of Moses, the following principles became clear to me: that if applied, God can turn anybody's life into a wonder for His glory. God has perfect timing, never early, never late. You were born at the right time.

When we think of Moses, it can be challenging to relate to his life if we focus on burning bushes, plagues, and parted seas. However, when we remember that he was imperfect, just like us, who needed God's guidance and strength, it becomes easier to see the principles and lessons we can learn from him and apply to our lives to maximize our potential and serve our generation.

A principle is a rule, belief, or idea that guides you.

Before we come to those principles, let's quickly look at Moses' life.

Acts 7:20 says, **"At that time Moses was born, and he was no ordinary child. For three months he was cared for by his family."**

Moses was born when the Hebrew children were being murdered by their oppressors, at the time enslaved by the Pharaoh of Egypt.

Moses' parents put him in a basket and sent him down a river, believing God to protect him. By God's intervention, he was adopted by the Pharaoh's daughter. After spending 40 years in the palace, he had to make faith decisions, which shaped what he became. Along the way, he made mistakes which resulted in killing an Egyptian, and this forced him to run away from Egypt. (Exodus 2:1-15)

While in the land in Midian, Moses married and became a shepherd, and while there, God appeared to him in the form of a burning bush. His encounter with God transformed his life and gave him a new direction. He returned and brought plagues to the slave masters before rescuing God's people. While not a perfect man, he led a life we can learn from.

Hebrews 11:24-26: **"By faith Moses, when he was grown up, refused to be called the son of Pharaoh's daughter, choosing rather to be mistreated by the people of God than to enjoy the fleeting pleasures of sin. He considered the reproach of Christ greater wealth than the treasures of Egypt, for he was looking to the reward."**

Inspiration from the life of Moses:

God knows you by name. (Exodus 3:1-4). He knows your past, location, and condition.

You were born in and for this generation. Every encounter with God demands a response from you. Moses' first response was to make excuses.

Results won't come easy. (Exodus 5:1-2). After He met with God and confronted Pharaoh, the dictator did not give in right away. That means you must be persistent in doing the right thing.

Get alone with God. (Exodus 3:1-4). Moses often got alone to pray and hear from God.

We must believe. (Exodus 4:10-17). Moses tried to excuse his way out of God's calling on His life. Regardless of your limitations, God will not abandon you in your calling.

Get help. (Exodus 18:13-14). Moses was not just a prophet. He was a leader, a lawmaker, a military commander, a judge, a spiritual leader, and so much more. But he needed help, and his father-in-law Jethro encouraged him to get help.

To live a significant life, you will need help. It's your responsibility to discern who your helpers are. God still helps people through people. You don't have to know much about the Bible, to know that Moses was a key player on God's team. Yet, there came a moment when Moses needed help.

In Exodus 17, we see two men holding up the weary arms of a man whose strength has been depleted.

In that story, the Israelites had been attacked and went to battle with their attackers. Moses stood at the top of the hill and held his staff in the air. This battle plan must have come by revelation, and it worked. Revelations change situations.

If Moses held the staff raised, Israel had the advantage. But as soon as he dropped his arms to rest, the advantage shifted to the enemy.

If you've ever had to hold your arms up high for any length of time, you know that they get tired quickly, even if your hands are empty.

Do a little experiment: Grab something around you and stand, holding it above your head for as long as possible.

You probably didn't even try it, but it doesn't take long for the weight to wear you down to the point that you can't do it anymore.

Fortunately for Moses, his two companions recognized that he needed help.

"Moses' arms became so tired he could no longer hold them up. So, Aaron and Hur found a stone for him to sit on. Then they stood on each side of Moses, holding up his hands. So, his hands held steady until sunset. As a result, Joshua overwhelmed the army of Amalek in battle." (Exodus 17:12-13)

YOU NEED HELP:

To live a significant life, you will need help.

There are many lessons from this story that are still relevant to you and me today.

Even one as great as Moses needed the help of others. It's always teamwork that brings victory.

It was his sister Miriam who suggested to Pharaoh's daughter that she could find a woman to take care of baby Moses. (Ex 2:7-9)

You are alive today because God has used several people to help you for His purposes. God placed people in Moses' life at this crucial time who could help in his time of need.

Not only does God provide people to help us, but He also places each of us in positions to help others. Supporting roles in the kingdom of God are just as important as the starring roles.

Not everyone is called to be a Moses, but we can all be Miriam, Aaron, or Hur. Whose hands are you supporting?

There will be times when we face a burden that is too heavy to bear alone. God can get us through any situation, but we must cooperate with His provision, which is often through people.

Aaron and Hur recognized the need and responded. Help is only effective if it is accepted.

Refusing needed help indicates pride in our lives that should be confessed and addressed. Aaron and Hur helped Moses throughout the battle without taking a break or complaining.

While looking at Moses, we can think about another example of two arms that grew weary from the weight they were carrying: the arms of Jesus, whose hands were secured to the cross with nails.

Arms and hands that carried the total weight of our sins. A weight that only he could bear. For He alone saved us because we could not save ourselves. Because of His sacrifice, we each should now raise our own hands in praise of His name.

His victory became ours when we accepted Him as Savior and Lord.

"God was with Moses." (Exodus 15:1-21).

This portion of Scripture is a song of praise for all God did. Moses and his sister Miriam sang it to thank Him for all He did. God led and fought for His people, and He will do the same for those who believe in Him.

Chapter 2

THE M.O.S.E.S PRINCIPLE
MASTER PLAN, OBEDIENCE, SACRIFICE, EMPOWERMENT, SUCCESS and STEWARDSHIP.

While there is pressure from society to succeed and meet a certain standard that the world holds us to, through God's calling on our lives, we can still be what He wants for our lives.

The Bible discusses God's plan and purpose for us and practically shows us how to live according to His purpose. The quality of your life is your number one priority, but it's only up to you to make it a purposeful journey of faith in God. You must build a lifestyle of faith in God to enjoy life fully.

Do you often feel frustrated in particular areas of your life?

Waking up each day to the same painful repetitive cycle that seems never-ending? Has the quality of your life decreased over time, in particular areas, resulting in a loss of energy, vitality, and enthusiasm for the future?

Life can be overwhelming, even for those who know what God wants them to be and do with their lives. The tough times can seem overbearing without understanding where our lives are headed and why they're headed there.

Usually, ignorance of purpose, especially during trials, causes many to abuse or misuse their lives and opportunities.

We should focus on knowing God, ourselves, our enemy, and our place in God's plan.

Stay focused on the right things daily and avoid those that make you feel down. Be the best version of yourself daily, and never stop growing.

It was Moses' sacrifice of laying down the pleasures of the palace that is still blessing us to eternity.

Hebrews 6:12: **"We do not want you to become lazy, but to imitate those who through faith and patience inherit what has been promised."**

The above scripture talks about how those who came before us obtained promises through faith and patience. We are encouraged to imitate them. To imitate means to take or follow as a model.

Moses' parents faced a dilemma when he was only three months old. Pharoah had ordered that every make Hebrew must be killed at birth or thrown in the river. The parents could only hide him for three months.

"But when she could hide him no longer, she got a papyrus basket for him and coated it with tar and pitch. Then she placed the child in it and put it among the reeds along the bank of the Nile." (Exodus 2:3)

As Bible readers, we are blessed to know the end of the story. We learn how Moses spent forty years in the palace of the very leader who wanted him dead and how he became a leader, deliverer, lawgiver, prophet, singer, intercessor, military man, but above all, a friend of God.

For Moses to become what he became, it was God's providence and faith-based choices.

The Bible commends the faith of Moses' parents and his choices of faith.

FAITH HOLDS GREATER VALUES. (Hebrews 11:24-26)

Moses' generation lived under Egypt's disfavor.

What began as a harmonious relationship between the kings of Egypt and the family of Jacob turned into bitter envy against God's people.

Moses was a Hebrew living inside the Egyptian power structure.

Like Moses, God has preserved your life because you have a place in His master plan for this generation. You are responsible for making faith choices; seek Him, develop your gifts, and deploy them to help others.

When Moses grew up, he refused to be called the son of Pharaoh's daughter. *Refused* is a word that indicates a specific choice, a moment likely backed by much deliberation and consideration.

16

With premeditated thought, Moses came to the point of decision where he removed himself from Pharaoh's family.

A Jewish historian, Josephus, accurately depicted Moses' secular life. He said Moses was the crown prince of Pharaoh, a mighty general who'd won significant battles for Egypt.

Moses was a hero.

Growing up as the grandson of Pharaoh in Egypt's most glorious days would've had great advantages, but he decided to lay it all down.

Moses knew his identity and as a Hebrew, he chose to **"be mistreated with the people of God."**

Had we been there, we might have tried to talk him out of it, but Moses made the right decision.

Today, eternity rejoices over his life. So do we.

He pursued what made his heart sad and wanted to be the solution. A moment came when he began calculating life differently. He considered Christ's shame or disgrace **"greater wealth"** than all the **"treasures of Egypt."** What a way to look at life!

In all this, Moses **"was looking to the reward,"** and God granted it.

First, he got a front-row seat to God's workings on earth. Second, he received an incredible legacy; he became God's instrument. Third, he gained eternity with God. Fourth, he entered a friendship with God. Fifth, he was a part of God's winning team, for Israel to overcome Egypt's oppression through the power of God.

Faith will always rearrange our value system.

Faith enables us to avoid dishonest forms of income and get the pleasure of God upon our work. It helps us value our integrity more than dishonesty increases. It strengthens us to resist sexual desires God forbids in favor of his eternal reward.

Society continuously makes us think that the entertainment we consume, the degrees we accumulate, or the friends we acquire are all there is to life. Moses made the hard choice and laid down his life to pursue God's plan and purpose.

The faith Moses displayed is of great aid to us as believers. Your stand for Christ and His word will get you embarrassment, but it is worth the shame when you consider the reward.

One day, after you let Him rearrange your value system and live according-ly, He'll say, **"Well done, good and faithful servant, enter into the joy of your Master"** [see Matthew 25:21].

Always remember:

1. God has a master plan for everybody and can and will use any body who believes. (Exodus 2:1-3; Hebrews 11:23). You were born in this generation and for your generation. (Acts 7:20). You must trust God, no matter how hopeless things seem.

2. God can use you, no matter where you come from. (Ex. 2:4-10). God transformed Moses went from a pauper to a prince.

3. Even those called by God will make mistakes. (Exodus 2:11-12, Numbers 20:8) Moses reacted in anger by killing an Egyptian when he tried to defend an Israelite.

4. Embrace your calling. (Exodus 3:4-10). Moses was initially hesitant, pushing back with 'buts' and 'what ifs.' Eventually, he embraced his calling and trusted God.

5. Repentance brings restoration, no matter how serious your sins are. (Exodus 2:13-14).

6. God can use you when you prioritize Him over your pleasures. (Exodus 2:15; Mark 8:34;Philippians 3:7). Do you value God more than your wealth and worldly accomplishments?

7. God can use you when you live in the world, but not when you are in the world. (Exodus 2:16-22).

8. God is looking for you to free others still in bondage. (Exodus 2:23-25). The word *remember* meant that God turned His attention to them as their predicted 400-year captivity was coming to an end.

9. Have faith. (Exodus14:13-26). When the Israelites were seemingly trapped between the Red Sea and the pursuing Egyptian army, Moses had faith and told them to stand firm and watch God save them. As we face struggles and our own

'Red Sea' moments, let our faith in God bring assurance that he will deliver us.

10. Stay humble. (Numbers 12:3). We must stay humble before God and each other, even when we are in positions of power and influence.

11. Don't try to do it all on your own. (Exodus 18:13). He 'listened to his father-in-law and did everything he said' (verse 24)

12. Seek God's will. (Numbers 21:6-9). When the people acknowledged that they had sinned, Moses prayed for God's will. Afterward, God instructed Moses to make a bronze snake and put it on a pole. Then, when anyone was bitten by a snake and looked at the bronze snake, they lived.

What we should do in challenging circumstances is not always obvious, but we must remember to seek God's will for a solution. The instructions might not always make much sense to us, but miracles will always happen when we follow His instructions by faith.

AN INTENTIONAL GOD DEMANDS THAT WE LIVE OUR LIVES INTENTIONALLY.

God is always intentional about where we find ourselves. You may or may not like where you are, but God knows and can turn an ordinary day of your life into an extraordinary one. He can turn a day of calamity into a day of celebration in a moment. That's what happened when, all of a sudden, a princess showed up right on time, and through a series of events, Moses' mother was paid from the palace to raise Moses. I believe God gave the parents another chance to instill faith and God's values in Moses.

"Moses was educated in all the wisdom of the Egyptians and was powerful in speech and action. When Moses was forty years old, he decided to visit his own people, the Israelites. He saw one of them being mistreated by an Egyptian, so he went to his defense and avenged him by killing the Egyptian." (Acts 7:22-24)

From the above text, we can conclude that God will use our path to prepare us for our Kingdom purpose.

To live intentionally means that we make deliberate and purposeful decisions. It means thinking ahead and making choices based on your personal values, beliefs and goals.

God had a plan for you, and He chose you. (Ephesians 1:4-5, 13)

God uses the Holy Spirit to build our lives, allowing us to function in the world we live in today for His glory. He made you for good works. (Ephesians 2:10).

This is how we are to live our lives intentionally:

- Walk worthy of your calling. (Ephesians 4:1). Paul turns from belief to behavior.
- Be renewed in the spirit of your mind. Our head, heart, hands, thinking, emotions, and behavior can either be under the authority of the Holy Spirit, or they can be under our control.
- Work with your own hands. (Ephesians 4:28)

21

- Use your time wisely (Ephesians 5:16). Time is precious. Today, we occupy our time with many distractions and do not use the time God has given us profitably. We get about 27,000 days on the planet (Psalm 90:12). Nothing is more valuable than using the time to reach someone for Christ.
- Be filled with the Spirit (Ephesians 5:18). There's power when we humbly ask the spirit of God to direct us in how we will live our lives every day.
- Work as unto the Lord (Ephesians 6:7). Ultimately, what we do for God matters.

Chapter 3

God's Master Plan

"For we are God's masterpiece. He has created us anew in Christ Jesus, so we can do the good things he planned for us long ago." (Ephesians 2:10 NLT)

"No, we neither make nor save ourselves. God does both the making and saving. He creates each of us by Christ Jesus to join him in the work he does, the good work he has gotten ready for us to do, work we had better be doing. A master pierce is a work done, with extraordinary skill. According to the above text, you have His fingerprints on you." (Ephesians 2:10 MSG)

Much of what God made was through a spoken word. But He formed you with His hands and breathed into you His life. That's how special you and

I are before Him.

God has a master plan for the world and wants you to fit in it. That's what it means when we talk about purpose.

God formed you, so He could delight in you as His gift to your generation.

"For I know the thoughts that I think towards you, saith the Lord, thoughts of good and not of evil, and to give you an expected end." (Jeremiah 29:11)

According to the above scripture, God's thoughts towards us are of good and not of evil.

No matter what the case may be, His plans for you will come to pass as you obey His word.

From a human perspective, we often worry about what the future holds for us, but worry is always a sign of unbelief. Whenever you feel overwhelmed, speak to your soul; **"...bless the Lord all my soul and forget not all His benefits."** (Psalm 103:1-5).

Whenever you allow Satan to silence you, you are opening yourself to depression.

GOD HAS A MASTER PLAN FOR THE WORLD:

God's Master Plan is to fill the earth with His glory, and He wants to do it through you. **"But as truly as I live all the earth shall be filled with the glory of the LORD."** (Numbers 14:21)

Here, God tells Moses about His plan for the earth; one day, the whole earth will be filled with His glory. **"For the earth will be filled with the knowledge of the glory of the LORD, as the waters cover the sea."** (Habakkuk 2:14)

God plans to use you and me to accomplish His plan on earth. That's why it's important for us to know where we fit in His plan and use our spheres of influence accordingly.

God has given each person a unique set of skills and passions. It's up to each of us to discover what they are and use them, not only for our benefit but also for the benefit of those around us.

You are free to live your life as it feels best to honor God. God has a plan for you, but instead of waiting for a specific calling, identify your passions and use them for His glory.

You have freedom in His plan, and God's Word gives you guidelines and boundaries.

Ways to Follow God's Plan for Your Life:

As a Bible reader, you know you are familiar with Jeremiah 29:11, but let's look at some other key Bible verses about God's plan for our lives.

Jesus summed up God's commands for us: love God, love your neighbor. (Matthew 22:37-40)

God plans for every person to come, to know Him, and to walk with Him. (2 Peter 3:9, Galatians 5:16)

God's plan is for you to do good works with the gifts He's given you. (Ephesians 2:10)

Specific things you can know about God's plan for all:

(1) God's plan is for his people to be reunited with him. That's the central message of the Bible. God's plan for you centers around the lost being found.

   -How are you using your influence and affluence to win the lost?

(2) God's plan is for us to have our basic needs met.

   -Every good father wants His children to have what they need.

(3) God's plan is for us to show his love to those around us.

   -This is through our prayers, words, and actions. We show His love by feeding the hungry, clothing the naked, and providing for those in need.

TO FIT IN HIS PLAN, DEMANDS:

1. WALKING WITH GOD: This means taking time each day to read His Word, worship, witness and doing warfare.

2. DYING TO YOURSELF: We are far too quickly pleased with food, power, money, and sex. Our desires will always let us down and leave us wanting more. But when we die to those desires, we can grab hold of something greater. (John 3:3-7, Matthew 16:24-26)

3. LIVING IN A COMMUNITY OF FAITH: You can only step fully into God's purpose and plan for your life with the help of others. Seek out a

godly community that will hold you accountable and be able to give you godly counsel.

4. LOVING THOSE AROUND YOU: You cannot love God and hate those around you. (Matthew 22:37-40). You are always in a unique spot to make an impact on someone in a way that no one else can.

5. DEVELOPING A CONSISTENT PRAYER AND FASTING LIFE STYLE.
   The power of prayer is in its consistency until you see the results. People like Hannah, Elijah, the early church, and Jesus Himself are great exam ples of the power of consistent prayer (Luke 18:1, 1 Thessalonians 5:17).

6. FOLLOW THE COMMANDS HE PUTS ON YOUR HEART.
   Allow God to guide your steps and trust the dreams He puts on your heart. "In all your ways submit to him, and he will make your paths straight." (Proverbs 3:6)

7. OBEY THE TRUTH: He will walk alongside you and aid you in your shortcomings as you walk in obedience. "If you are willing and obedient, you will eat the good things of the land; but if you resist and rebel, you will be devoured by the sword." For the mouth of the Lord has spoken." (Isaiah 1:19-20)

Chapter 4

Obedience!

The next pillar of a satisfying life is obedience. John 14:15 says, **"If you love me, obey my commandments."**

In both Greek and Hebrew, it means attentive hearkening, compliance, or submission.

Obedience is hearing God's word and acting accordingly.

Our obedience to God through His word determines the depth of our relationship with him and the level of divine interventions in our lives.

God calls us to develop the "Yes" Habit whenever He speaks. This will enable us to watch out for what God is doing now and get in alignment with

Him.

This lifestyle gives us greater sensitivity to discern the voice of God.

Obedience comes from successful listening and is proof of our love for God.

Luke 6:46 says, **"Why do you call me, 'Lord, Lord,' and do not do what I say?"** According to the above Scripture, it's possible to call Him Lord and yet live a disobedient life.

God's promises when we are obedient:

"If ye be willing and obedient, ye shall eat the good of the land: But if ye refuse and rebel, ye shall be devoured with the sword: for the mouth of the Lord hath spoken it." (Isaiah 1:19-20). According to the above text, you can choose to eat the good of the land or to be eaten.

"Now if you obey me fully and keep my covenant, then out of all nations you will be my treasured possession. Although the whole earth is mine." (Exodus 19:5). What in life can you compare with being a treasured possession of the Almighty God!

"If you fully obey the Lord your God and carefully follow all his commands I give you today, the Lord your God will set you high above all the nations on earth. All these blessings will come on you and accompany you if you obey the Lord your God." (Deuteronomy 28:1-2) The blessings are conditional from the above text and all the way through verse 14.

Obedience is the meter key that unlocks Kingdom blessings.

"If you keep my commands, you will remain in my love, just as I have kept my Father's commands and remain in his love." (John 15:10). Obedience is what keeps us in His love, which will enable us to love others unconditionally.

"But whoever looks intently into the perfect law that gives freedom and continues in it not forgetting what they have heard, but doing it, they will be blessed in what they do." (James 1:25)

All these are incredible promises to obedient people, but Satan will fight to make sure that we do not obey God. We can choose to obey or disobey Him.

THE BENEFITS OF LIVING IN OBEDIENCE:

Obedience brings blessings, attracts favor with God and man, brings healing, leads to prosperity, leads to deliverance, conquers failure, and brings miracles.

Read and study the following scriptures. (Genesis 12:1-3, 39:2-4, 2 Kings 5:1-14, Job 36:11, Exodus14:21-22, Luke 5:1-10, I Kings 17:8-16)

(1) Obedience will make you a channel for miracles.

(2) Through obedience, you will know His ways.

(3) Obedience will enable us to develop boldness. Your faith will not stay at the same level when you obey God. Simon answered, **"Master, we've worked hard all night and haven't caught anything. But because you say so, I will let down the net. When they had done so, they caught such a large number of fish that their**

nets began to break. So, they signaled their partners in the other boat to come and help them, and they came and filled both boats so full that they began to sink." (Luke 5:5-7)

From the above text, the reward of their obedience has become a generational testimony of encouragement. Your obedience will impact not only your life, but also the lives of those around you.

(4) Obedience enables us to become friends of God. (Exodus 33:11, Isaiah 41:8, James 2:23)

(5) Obedience is the source of true Joy. We get joy through obedience by keeping and acting on the Word of God by faith, trusting in God wholeheartedly, living in humility,studying and meditating on God's Word, sponsoring God's work with our resources and other financial commitments, living in love, and praying to God always.

Please read and study the following scriptures: (Hebrews 11:6, Psalm 125:1, 1 Peter 5:5-6, Joshua 1:8, Luke 6:38, 1 John 4:16, 1 Thessalonians 5:17)

BARRIERS TO OBEYING THE WORD

There are reasons why we can hear, but still fail to obey God.

Disobedience is the cause of instability and insecurity in people's lives. It's impossible to go through the storms of life successfully when you are not a doer of the word. (Matthew 7:24-27)

1. Procrastination. (Hebrews 3:15) Procrastination is one of Satan's

weapons to limit us. As long as you keep delaying obeying the word, you will also delay your blessings. Timing is critical in Kingdom matters. Promptness is the procrastination cure. What are you putting off for tomorrow?

2. Excuses. (Proverbs 20:4) Excuses will exclude you from God's promises and blessings.

3. Ignorance. (Hosea 4:6, John 8:32) You cannot practice what you don't know. Get to know the word of God and put the word to work in your life.

4. Fear of men. (Proverbs 29:25, Luke 6:26) Many people would instead flow with the opinions of men, then what God is saying. "But Peter and the apostles answered, "We must obey God rather than men." (Acts 5:29)

5. Lack of understanding. (Matthew 13:19, Luke 24:45) It isn't easy to practice what you don't understand.

6. Lack of courage. (Joshua 1:7) We cannot succeed if we do not learn the secret of how to draw courage from the Word.

7. Indecision. (1 Kings 18:21) You must make a conscious decision to practice the word, irrespective of circumstances and the opinions of men.

Chapter 5

Living a Life of Sacrifice

Outstanding achievement is usually born of great sacrifice and is never the result of selfishness.

There are three things you can do with your life: waste it by living selfishly, wreck it by living sinfully or give your life away by living sacrificially.

T.C. Studd said, *"Only one life will soon be past; only what's done for Christ will last."*

We can sacrifice in the areas of talent, time, and treasure.

Sacrifice must be a priority when it comes to Kingdom matters. God commands us to offerourselves as living sacrifices. It's the only way to become vessels of honor before Him.

To be "a living sacrifice" is to be entirely at God's disposal. It means you are available to obey whatever God asks or commands.

Living a life of sacrifice will cost us, but the benefits here and in eternity are worth it.

"Neither will I offer burnt offerings unto the LORD my God of that which doth cost me nothing." (2 Samuel 24:24)

As you may know from the story, King David had sinned against God. His wrong choices as a leader affected those that he led, and thousands of people died. As a broken man over his sins, he prayed that God punished him and not the people. God, in His mercy, instructed him to build an altar and make a sacrifice. He came across a generous man willing to give him the place and sacrifice. David knew it would only be effective if it were costing him something. It was this sacrifice that stopped the plague.

Sacrifice always does that for us. As the love for self-will has increased, people have reduced their commitment to the things of God and one another. We must know that our private and public choices will affect our relationship with God and those around us.

It's healthy to examine ourselves by asking a few questions:
- What is your motivation for service to God?
- Is it convenience or conviction?
- Can God truly depend on you to serve Him, whether it is convenient or not?

Some people serve God only when it is convenient. For some people, the blessings they get after prayer, which becomes the reason why they are no longer available to God.

WHY DO WE SACRIFICE?

(1) Jesus modeled the life of sacrifice (John 15:13). Our lives ought not to be dearer to us than Jesus' life was to Him.

(2) Sacrifice yields eternal rewards. (Mat 5:12) Life on earth is not our home. Your treasures lead your heart.

(3) Satan can't take what you give away to God. When you give something to God, it leaves your hand but not your life.

(4) Sacrifice helps to bring salvation. Our salvation is only possible be cause of the sacrifice of Jesus. We can't secure anyone's salvation by sacrificing, but others can hear about Jesus by our sacrifice.

(5) Sacrifice changes you. Sacrifice in our finances and other areas stretches our faith and our minds. Every Christian should be willing to sacrifice anything for Jesus Christ.

(6) We gain both present and future blessings. **"We have left everything to follow you."** (Luke 18:28-30). From the above text, Peter focused on what they had lost. Jesus' response: **"A hundred times as much..."** **"many times more..."** (Mark 10:30) Jesus's focus and response were on GAIN.

(7) We gain the kingdom and eternal life. **"Do not be afraid, little flock,**

for your Father has been pleased to give you the kingdom."
(Luke 12:32). We must be willing to give all to God to GAIN the
kingdom. (Matthew 13:44-46)

God's Kingdom can be experienced both in the present and the future.

THE REWARD OF SACRIFICING:

I read a story about an express package mailed from England to South Africa
many years ago. Postage was due upon delivery, but the recipient wouldn't
pay the fee. For about fourteen years, the box remained unclaimed and was
used as a footstool in the express office. After the consignee died, the box
and other unclaimed packages were auctioned and sold for nearly nothing.
When the purchaser opened it, he discovered several thousand pounds of
sterling English bank notes!

Because its recipient wouldn't sacrifice a nominal delivery fee, he forfeited
a fortune!

How often do we make this mistake, too? God delivers a blessing, but we
reject it because it requires a sacrifice. All along, God intends to leave a
blessing far richer than our sacrifice! This principle is presented throughout
the Bible.

God's blessing is always greater than our sacrifice!

Sacrifices Cost the Giver

An acceptable sacrifice is something that contains value. A sacrifice isn't
something we have no use for, and we offer it to God. That's called, *taking*

out the trash! God rewards us when we surrender what is precious.

God demonstrated the ultimate sacrifice of eternity when He surrendered his only begotten Son to death on the Cross. Nothing will ever surpass that!

Examples of people who sacrificed:

1. Abraham. (Gen 12:1-3, 22:1-3). God required him to leave his region, family, religion, and friends, and he did. God asked Abraham to place Isaac on the altar of sacrifice. Without hesitation, Abraham went to the mountain, built an altar, tied up his son, and drew back his knife. Suddenly, an angel of God commanded him to stop. God provided a lamb.

2. Moses. He was raised in the luxuries of Pharaoh's palace. But when he **'came of age'** Moses renounced kinship with Pharaoh and chose to suffer with Israel. Egypt's wealth and, eventually, the throne could have been his, but he rejected them. God rewarded Moses' sacrifice. (Hebrews 11:24-27)

3. David. (1 Chronicles 29:2-5). One scholar estimated that David contributed over three billion dollars to the temple construction. Our sacrifices touch God's heart and move his hand! (Psalms 126)

The secret of the early church's success was that the apostles and believers laid down their lives for Whom they believed.

"...men who have risked their lives for the name of our Lord Jesus Christ." (Acts 15:26)

These were men who risked their lives for the name of our Lord Jesus Christ.

We reap in proportion to our sowing. (Luke 6:38, 1 Corinthians 9:6-8)

Chapter 6

David Was a Man of Sacrifice

God testified about David as a man after His heart.

"But now your kingdom shall not endure. The Lord has sought for Himself aman after His own heart, and the Lord has appointed him ruler over His people, because you have not kept what the Lord commanded you." (1 Samuel 13:14)

Circumstances that preceded this declaration: (1 Samuel 13:8-13)

Saul, the first king of Israel, did well at the beginning. But it did not take long for his pride to grow and his reliance on God to fade.

When Saul and his army were under attack, he took matters into his own hands and made the offering himself.

1. He had received an express command to wait seven days.
2. He knew the stake of his kingdom depended on him waiting.
3. He was impatient and didn't trust God because of the pressure he was under. He chose to take matters into his own hands and make the burnt offering himself.
4. He made excuses rather than repenting When called out for this disobedience.

This disobedience by Saul was the beginning of his downfall. His pride, arrogance, and disobedience continued to grow. Saul would try to make up for his lack of obedience and trust in God by making burnt offerings, but God knew his heart. (1 Samuel 15:22)

Because of his disobedience, arrogance, lack of faith, and refusal to trust in the Lord, God rejected Saul as king, and David was chosen.

What Made David Different from Saul?

God knew David's heart and what he could do long before David knew his future.

We see his heart by looking at how he lived his life.

1. David's faith and sacrifice. (2 Samuel 24:24)
2. David's courage: Facing a sword-wielding giant with nothing but a sling and some rocks took courage. Before throwing the stone that would take the giant down, David declared: **"this entire assembly may know that the Lord does not save by sword or by spear; for the battle is the**

Lord's, and He will hand you over to us!" (1 Samuel 17:47) David credited God with defeating Goliath before the giant was hit by the stone. This giant-killing faith remained with David his entire life.

3. David's Trust. Even though Saul was a constant threat to his life, David respected him as king and spared his life on more than one occasion. When David could kill Saul in a cave, he chose not to. (1 Samuel 24:12-13) David knew that God had proclaimed him the next king, but unlike Saul with the burnt offering, he would wait until God removed Saul rather than take the matter into his own hands.

4. David's Love. (2 Samuel 9:1) In all his dealings with Saul, David showed agape love toward the man who was determined to be his enemy. (Matthew 5:44.)

5. David's Humility. After experiencing remarkable success in battle, David remained humble. (1 Samuel 18:23, 2 Samuel 7:18) At this point, David had known immense success at everything he put his hand to, yet he never took the credit or considered himself worthy of greatness.

6. David's Integrity. (1 Samuel 22:9-19) David admitted when he was wrong and took responsibility for his mistakes, which was a sign of his deep integrity.

7. David's brokenness and forgiveness. (Psalm 51) He slept with Bathsheba and then he had her husband murdered. David was distressed when the prophet Nathan revealed the terrible thing David had done. Instead of making excuses for his behavior, David said, **"I have sinned against the Lord."** (2 Samuel 12:2)

8. David Worships God. It is believed that David also wrote Psalms 32 at about the same time as Psalms 51.

Many of David's psalms were full of his heartaches and even questioning of God, but he never stopped serving and worshiping Him.

It's always healthy to ask ourselves some questions:

- Do we have faith and trust the Lord in all circumstances?
- Do we have sacrificial love for others, even our enemies?
- Are we humble?
- Do we operate with integrity?
- Do we seek forgiveness from God for our sins?
- Do we worship the Lord no matter the circumstances?

These are the qualities that make us people after God's heart.

True Faith and Sacrifice Go Together.

"But my righteous one will live by faith; and if he draws back, I have no pleasure in him." (Hebrews 10:38)

In the Bible, people of faith required immense sacrifice to live victorious lives.

I believe that God will not require less from us if we are to maximize our potential in this journey of faith.

We live in times when itching ears are more easily satisfied than ever. There are so many preachers of the Gospel proclaiming that if you love Jesus, you don't have to give up anything you have or are doing. And that you can have your best life, even if you don't surrender fully to His lordship. His grace is enough.

The Bible recognizes no faith that does not lead to obedience, nor does it recognize any obedience that does not spring from faith.

"The two are opposite sides of the same coin." - A.W. Tozer

[Read Hebrews 11:17-40]

Living by faith calls us to step out of our comfort zones to a zone of commitment where sacrifice and miracles occur.

Abraham-

Abraham lived an obedient lifestyle. (Genesis 12:1-3, 22:9-10)

Stepping out in faith is not a path of perfection but of brokenness and sacrifice.

Abraham stepped out in faith when God called him, but he did not always do it right.

"Wasn't Abraham our father justified by works in offering Isaac his son on the altar? You see that faith was active together with his works, and by works, faith was made complete, and the Scripture was fulfilled that says, Abraham believed God, and it was credited to him as righteousness, and he was called God's friend." (James 2:21–24)

You see, a person is justified by works and not by faith alone. The above verses reveal to us that you cannot separate a life of faith from sacrifice. We can believe all we want, but if our faith in God does not motivate us to sacrifice, that faith is shallow.

Bible patriarchs like Isaac, Jacob, and Joseph faced great challenges in confident faith. They trusted, submitted, believed, and obeyed God. Their journeys had many trials, but their testimonies outweighed their trials because they understood sacrifice.

God accomplishes great things on behalf of those who sacrifice faithfully.

Stories of people like Daniel, who shut the mouth of Lions in Daniel 6, also of the three Hebrew boys who quenched the raging fire in Daniel 3 are very inspiring.

Generational testimonies are birthed when we learn the principle of sacrifice.

Abraham realized that everything he had was because of God and that everything he had, including his son, was God's.

Sadly, some faith is all talk and never leads to action.

"Then he said to them all, "If anyone wants to follow after me, let him deny himself, take up his cross daily, and follow me." (Luke 9:23)

Sacrificing for Christ is always a challenge, as our lives are riddled with distractions, desires, opinions, and worldly thoughts that tell us sacrificing to follow Jesus isn't worth it.

"Therefore, through him let us continually offer up to God a sacrifice of praise, that is, the fruit of lips that confess his name. Don't neglect to do what is good and to share, for God is pleased with such sacrifices." (Hebrews 13:15-16)

We care far too much about what others think of us instead of letting God's word motivate us.

The cost was significant and has continued to be great to those who live a life of impact for the Kingdom.

By faith, we must keep this message going by our obedience and sacrifice.

This message of hope and faith in Jesus is worth proclaiming, and it's worth sacrificing for.

Chapter 7

What Is In Your Hands?

This question appears for the first time in Exodus 4:2, where God called Moses and told him to go and lead the children of Israel into the Promised Land.

When Moses feared the Hebrews wouldn't believe him, God asked him, **'What is in your hand?'** To Moses, it was just a staff used to beat stubborn sheep, but to God, it was the instrument by which miracles would be performed.

The staff in Moses' hands became the staff of God (Exodus 4:20), and it was used to perform the ten plagues, part the Red Sea, bring water out of the rock, etc.

In John 6: 5-12, Jesus wanted to feed over 5000 people who had gathered to hear him speak.

They did not have enough to buy the needed food, but a boy offered five loaves of bread and two fish. To the disciples, five loaves of bread and two fish couldn't feed 5000 people, but to God, it was more than enough. Jesus blessed and broke the little put in His hands, and it was enough with 12 baskets of leftovers.

Examples of God using ordinary things in the hands of those He called:

"The Lord said, "Throw it on the ground." Moses threw it on the ground, and it became a snake, and he ran from it." (Exodus 4:3)

"After Ehud came Shamgar son of Anath, who struck down six hundred Philistines with an ox goad. He too saved Israel." (Judges 3:31)

"And David put his hand in his bag and took out a stone and slung it and struck the Philistine on his forehead. The stone sank into his forehead, and he fell on his face to the ground." (1 Samuel 17:49)

"Finding a fresh jawbone of a donkey, he grabbed it and struck down a thousand men." (Judges 15:15)

The above verses encourage us to recognize and utilize our God-given resources and talents to advance God's kingdom and His glory.

Let us strive to be men and women of character, using our God-given resources not for our glory but for the advancement of His kingdom.

These passages remind us of the power and potential of our resources if only we would use them for His glory.

God works with what is in our hands. We often look outside ourselves for help to do something, and we doubt God's ability to use what he has placed in us. God can take our little and make it into something more than enough for us.

In 2 Kings 4:1- 7, the widow of a prophet was in debt and had no means of paying it. She went to Elisha for help. He asked her, **'What do you have in your house?' She replied, 'Nothing, just a little oil'.**

To her, that oil was nothing, but to God, it was what she needed to start with to meet her current needs. Elisha gave instructions, and the little oil-filled barrels were sold to cover her debts.

There are many such examples in the Bible when God used people's current abilities and possessions to bless them and increase their lot.

At every point in a person's life and destiny, there will always be something or someone available that God can use to bring the needed miracle.

What you will be and do will always come from what you already have.

"Because by his power he has given us everything necessary for life and righteousness." (2 Peter 1:3)

Do not despise what you have now; instead, recognize it, be grateful for it, nurture it with all your heart, speak the word of God into it, and watch God use it to increase you.

"Do not despise these small beginnings." (Zechariah 4:10)

We all have desires, aspirations, dreams, etc., and sometimes, they cause us to despise what we currently have. We hate our jobs, partners, houses, and clothes; everything about us seems to be what we don't need.

I pray that your eyes will be opened to the fact that God will use what you currently have to get you to where He needs you to be.

Nothing happens by chance; you are not in that current situation by chance; it's all part of a plan and supposed to work together for your good. But that can only happen if you stop despising and complaining about what you have and start seeing what God wants to do through it. (2 Corinthians 4:7, 1 Corinthians 1:27)

How do we turn what we have now into what we need it to be?

We need to find what God's Word says about that thing or situation first and then take the responsibility to practice the Word.

RECOGNIZING YOUR ASSETS:

An asset is a resource with economic value that an individual owns or controls with the expectation that it will provide a future benefit.

In our lives, we often feel like Moses. We feel inadequate and ill-equipped to do God's work.

We look at our lives, skills, and resources and think, "What can I do with these?"

But just as God used Moses' staff to perform miracles, He can use what's in our hands to do extraordinary things. We need to recognize what we have and be willing to use it by faith for His glory.

The staff in Moses' hand was a tool he used every day as a shepherd. It was familiar, something he knew how to use, and a part of his identity. And it was this ordinary, everyday object that God turned into a kingdom asset to perform extraordinary miracles.

God has placed certain gifts, talents, and resources in our hands. These are our assets. They may seem ordinary to us, just like the staff seemed ordinary to Moses. But when we recognize them and use them for God's glory, they can become extraordinary.

The first step in using your assets is recognizing what they are. What are your gifts and talents?

What resources do you have? These are not just physical things. They can be our time, skills, knowledge, relationships, experiences, passions, and abilities. These are things that God has given us that we can use for His glory.

Secondly, we need to be willing to use them. Moses had to throw his staff on the ground at God's instruction. He had to let go of it and surrender it to God. In the same way, we need to surrender our assets to God. We must be willing to use them for His purposes, not our own. This will require us to step out of our comfort zones, take risks, and trust God. When we take faith risks, we will see God do extraordinary things through us.

Thirdly, using our assets requires us to rely on God's power, not our own. When Moses threw his staff on the ground, it became a snake. When he picked it up, it became a staff again. It was not Moses' power that transformed the staff, but God's.

We must rely on Him, trust in His power, and believe He can do extraordinary things through us.

Finally, using our assets requires us to persevere. Moses faced many challenges and obstacles in leading the Israelites out of Egypt. He faced opposition from the Pharaoh, doubts from the Israelites, and even fears and insecurities.

But he persevered. He kept using what was in his hand, trusting in God's power, and following God's guidance.

Throughout the Scriptures, we find that the heroes of faith were ordinary people with ordinary resources who believed in God, and He used them in extraordinary ways.

Chapter 8

Empowerment!

Empowerment is authority or power given to someone to do something; it's also the process of becoming stronger and more confident.

All of us left by ourselves are like an empty glove or a balloon without air in it.

When God called Moses to perform the task, Moses did not feel capable of doing it. He initially focused on his limitations, not the one who called him.

1. The problem of personal inferiority.
    "Who am I?" This first excuse is the problem of personal inferiority. The issue was not who Moses was but who God was and is. "I will be with you" was God's response, and this is all you need. Are you

struggling with inferiority? Find your identity in God.

2. The problem with the message.

His second excuse was the problem of the message: "What shall I say?" "I AM THAT I AM" was the answer. Our God is a covenant-keeping God, and He will keep His word that He has made with Abraham, Isaac, and Jacob to whoever believes.

3. The problem of the reception.

A. Excuse: **"They will not believe me,"** Exodus 4:1. Exodus 3: 18, God said to Moses, **"They shall pay heed to what you say."** Moses' concern in verse 1, **"What if they will not believe me nor listen to what I say?"**

What are your difficulties and impossibilities? If God is between them and you, everything is fine. By faith, this will bring victory to you and glory to God. If your difficulties are between you and God, panic attacks will over-take you. This will produce fear, defeat, frustration, and misery.

Where God is concerning your difficulty makes all the difference in the world for you.

B. Answer, signs, and miracles. Moses had been rejected as a leader and deliverer by these people. (Acts 7:35-37). He felt like the same thing was going to happen. The Lord assured him of three signs whereby the people would know that the Lord had sent him.

Signs were to authenticate the man and the message (4:5). Whenever God commissioned a person, signs from the Lord accompanied them.

The first of the three signs:

(1) Rod: **"Throw down your staff"** (4:2-5.) **"What is that in your hand?"** It was a shepherd's staff.

The Lord would take this despised thing and person to do a work for Him. Moses was to carry this staff with him into Egypt and before Pharaoh.

This was similar to the Lord Jesus Christ: **"He was despised and forsaken of men; A man of sorrows, and acquainted with grief... He was despised, and we did not esteem him."** (Isaiah 53:3).

It was this despised one that the Lord would use to deliver His people.

Moses obeyed, and as the staff became a writhing serpent ready to strike and destroy, Moses became fearful. He didn't like snakes any better than you or I do.

"Stretch out your hand and grasp it by its tail." Moses obeyed the Lord's words exactly as He gave them, which became a staff in his hand.

This staff was no longer ordinary; the miracle-working power of God had transformed it. God is taking that which is nothing in the eyes of men and turning it into an u of power and usefulness.

What you have in your hands does not need to be something extraordinary. God wants to use that insignificant, ordinary thing that man sees as of no value if you believe.

"What is that in your hand?" For David, it was a sling, and five smooth stones yielded to God, and these became the means of blessing the nation of Israel and glorying the Lord, which continues to this day. (1Samuel 17:40)

"What is that in your hand?" Andrew said to the Lord, **"There is a lad here who has five barley loaves and two fish is but what are these among so many?"** (John 6:9)

"What are these among so many?" This is not the issue. It is who He is, not what it is that you have.

Someone may be saying, "I'm too old to serve the Lord." Abraham was 75 years old when the Lord called him, and Moses was 80 years old at the burning bush.

"What is that in your hand?" For Dorcas, it was good works in arms deeds that she did (Acts 9:36). God rewarded Dorcas by restoring her to life.

Moses may have thought that it would take the sword to deliver Israel out of Egypt, but God used the insignificant, worthless, despised item in the eyes of men.

Under the hand of God, an ordinary man with an ordinary rod became mighty to the pulling down the strongholds of the enemy.

In this generation, God wants you to be that rod in His hands, a channel of His miracles to deliver His people.

The Promised Power from On High:

A Christian girl was visiting from Eastern Europe, and her hosts asked her what impressions she had formed about the Churches she had visited in Britain. She said, "The church in England is like a great big factory—but the power is switched off!" The power is switched off—how different from the life of the Early Church.

"I am going to send you what my Father has promised; but stay in the city until you have been clothed with power from on high." (Luke 24:49)

The three keywords are *promise, wait,* and *power.*

In the O.T., we find the word "power" more than a hundred times, referring to the strength of individual men and women. In that sense, our human power can come from training, experience, human wisdom, or hard work. God calls us not to rely on our human power but on the power of His Holy Spirit.

"This is the word of the LORD to Zerubbabel: Not by might nor by power, but by my Spirit,' says the LORD Almighty." (Zechariah 4:6)

In the New Testament, the word we translate as power refers not to the strength of men and women, but to the power of the almighty God.

When Jesus promised his disciples **"power from on high,"** this was the kind of power He was talking about. The Greek word in question is *Dunamis,* and from that root, we get two significant English words. The first is dynamo, which generates electrical power. The second is dynamite, the explosive.

Jesus promised to give His disciples the power of the Holy Spirit, *dunamis,* the dynamo and the dynamite of the Christian life!

The source of this empowerment is an encounter with God. Every genuine encounter with God will change the recipient's destiny, and there will be marks to prove it.

Encountering God is much deeper than a tangible feeling or emotion. To experience God is to have your inner Spirit refined and redirected so that it completely changes your life. (Ephesians 3:19)

It means you discover who you were made to be and who He has always seen you as.

Can you think of a time when you experienced Him, and His presence completely changed your life?

"God is a consuming fire." (Hebrews 12:29). We know that what goes into a fire cannot come out unchanged.

These are some of the things that will happen in your life as you yield to God's presence:

1. God will reposition you on the straight path. **"Now get up and go into the city, and you will be told what you must do (Acts 9:6)." He will show you the way you should go in life.** (Psalm 143:8, Psalms 32:8). The Holy Spirit takes you from a place of darkness to ultimate light and salvation.

2. God will heal your heart. (Mathew 11:28) Forgiveness moves in, the feeling of loss and sorrow is consumed in peace and wholeness from the Father.

3. God will change your family and those closest to you. The godly life you live will impact those closest to you.

4. You will become an ambassador for Christ. (2 Corinthians 5:20, Romans 10:14-17, Romans 1:16). If you have encountered God, you have what everyone needs, and everyone needs what you have.

5. You will get the strength and power to break cycles of addictions. (1 John 3:6-7, 2 Corinthians 5:18-21) The presence of God is that of a refining fire. (Malachi 3:2-3)

6. You will have a great desire to build God's Kingdom. (Ph 4:17-19). Your heart will be given to reaching the lost, even if you do not physical -ly go to those places. (2 Corinthians 8:3-5).

7. You will hunger for His presence and Glory in every area of your life. (Psalm 63:1-8) You will Go from an encounter with God to constant fellowship with God. Fellowship means companionship, partnership, connection, and intimacy. (Isaiah 30:18) Our relationship and dependence upon Him will impact the way we steward what God has placed in our hands.

Have you had such an experience with God, or is your heart burning for such an experience?

The busier I become, the more I'm tempted to rush or even decrease my prayer time. But whenever I do this, I struggle in every area of life.

Not every prayer experience leaves me feeling like I've had a profound encounter with God.

Encounters with God will require patience and persistence. Effective encounters will involve 1) locating yourself, 2) responding to God, and 3) experiencing the fruits of the encounter.

Locating myself - In Genesis 3:9, God asked Adam: **"Where are you?"** Adam had just disobeyed God, and he covered his intimate parts with fig leaves and hid behind the trees. Adam's response to sin was to alienate himself from God. God did not expect to learn something new from Adam. God asked Adam this question to help him locate himself and develop the desire to come out of hiding.

In any honest encounter with God, you must identify where you are, what's on your mind, and what emotions you are experiencing. Become aware of your exhaustion, frustrations, fears, joy, and sadness. What question is God asking you today?

Responding to God - Adam responded honestly by telling God that he was afraid because he was naked, so he hid. Being 'naked' in front of God is scary.

Prophet Isaiah faced it in Isaiah 6

Adam had always been naked before God, and God didn't seem to mind before. Adam was the one who was suddenly aware of his nakedness and bothered by it.

God is merciful, but God is also intimidating. Approaching God requires both humility and courage. We need humility to look honestly at ourselves and the courage to stand, essentially naked, before God.

Humility asks me to stand in need of God's love and mercy. Courage requires vulnerability. This means a death of my will in favor of God's will. This will require change, and they will lead us to eternal life with God.

Are there resistances, fears, and challenges that you face as you think about encountering God?

The Fruits of An Encounter with God:

The "fruits" of an encounter with God aren't always what we would expect, and they aren't always pleasant or comfortable, but they are always for our good.

Encounter with God invites transformation. God gives us a new heart and a new spirit.

Can you imagine what could be the fruits of an encounter with God in your life?

There are certain things in this Kingdom that cannot be taught or preached; you have to just catch them.

"That I may know him, and the power of his resurrection, and the fellowship of his sufferings, being made conformable unto his death." (Philippians 3:10)

I pray that the Lord will instill in your soul a deep thirst and hunger to know Him, not by head knowledge but experientially.

As a generation, we need an encounter that will restore us to our place of relevance: to be the salt and light of the world because the standard has fallen so low (Matthew 5:13).

God loves to be pursued and sought after. He places a very high price on every encounter, and only when He senses a genuine hunger, and thirst can He reveal Himself. God is not a discovery; He is a revelation. (Isaiah 55:1)

We must not settle, relax, or think we have arrived. Psalms 42:3 says, **"My tears have been my food day and night, While they continually say to me, "Where [is] your God?"**

Situations, people, and the environment around you all question, 'Where is your God? Or is your God real? Is He alive?' We need God more than we think.

The Lord is inviting us to a higher level of fellowship, prayer, and communion, and walk with Him so that we can encounter Him and solve people's problems.

"If You treat me like this, please kill me here and now—if I have found favor in Your sight—and do not let me see my wretchedness!" (Numbers 11:15)

Moses was overwhelmed and asked God to take him away until God promised to show him His hand. This was the same Moses who had already seen such a mighty display of God's power.

Sometimes, we are bankrupt and empty, but instead of accepting, we put on a show of spirituality: I believe this is the reason the church is lacking.

We need an entirely fresh encounter with the Holy Spirit to be metamorphosed into what God wants us to be.

There must be a fresh understanding, longing, and craving for the person and ministry of the Holy Spirit in our individual lives before we can be used by Him and be a blessing. (1John 1:1-3)

These men reached a point where they held, felt, and experienced Him, and that's why they reached a point of surrendering all to and for Him. (2 Peter 1:16)

These are not man-made stories or fantasies; Peter told the church what he had witnessed.

"To every generation God reveals Himself." (Romans 2:11). The once timid apostles, who had hidden when Jesus was being crucified, were something else after the day of Pentecost when they encountered the Holy Spirit. (Acts 1:4)

May the Holy Spirit take us there. (Acts 3:19, Revelation 1:6, 2 Corinthians 3:17-18)

THREE MAJOR MANIFESTATIONS OF THE POWER:

1. Power for miracles of healing and deliverance.
   The Holy Spirit is the power source for accomplishing the great commission!

   The Ministry of Jesus:
   "Jesus returned to Galilee in the power of the Spirit, and news about

him spread.” (Luke 14:14)

“What is this teaching? With authority and power, he gives orders to evil spirits and they obey him.” (Luke 4:36)

“And the power of the Lord was present for him to heal.” (Luke 5:17)

“People touched him because power was coming from him and healing them all.” (Luke 8:46)

During His earthly ministry, Jesus passed that power on to his disciples, first to the 12 and then to the 72.

“When Jesus had called the Twelve together, he gave them power and authority to drive out all demons and to cure diseases, and he sent them out to preach the kingdom of God and to heal the sick.” (Luke 9:1, 2)

These miracles of healing and deliverance continued in the Early Church.

“Everyone was filled with awe, and many wonders and miraculous signs were done by the apostles.” (Acts 2: 43)

“Peter and John were enabled to heal the lame man sitting at the beautiful gate of the temple.” (Acts 3)

Miracles were a characteristic of the early church and a mark of many of those first Christians.

"Now Stephen, a man full of God's grace and power, did great won ders and miraculous signs among the people." (Acts 6:8)

"So Paul and Barnabas spent considerable time there, speaking boldly for the Lord, who confirmed the message of his grace by en- abling them to do miraculous signs and wonders." (Acts 14: 3)

"God did extraordinary miracles through Paul, so that even hand kerchiefs and aprons that had touched him were taken to the sick, and their illnesses were cured and the evil spirits left them." (Acts 19:11-12)

Power from on high is power for miracles, healing and deliverance. All the scriptures above should encourage us to pursue what authenticated the message of Jesus, His disciples, and the early church.

2. Power in proclaiming the gospel.
   Fuel is a necessity if you want to go anywhere! The Holy Spirt is the fuel for the engine of the great commission!

   "With great power the apostles continued to testify to the resurrection of the Lord Jesus, and much grace was upon them all." (Acts 4:33)

   "I am not ashamed of the gospel, because it is the power of God for the salvation of everyone who believes." (Romans 1:16)

   "My message and my preaching were not with wise and persuasive words, but with a demonstration of the Spirit's power." (1 Corinthians 2:4)

"…because our gospel came to you not simply with words, but also with power, with the Holy Spirit and with deep conviction." (1 Thessalonians 1:5)

Our part as believers is simply to make sure we are available to God, ready to obey Him and He will always provide the power.

3. Power to live the victorious Christian life.
   The Old Testament appearance of the phrase **"Power from on high"**:

"The fortress will be abandoned, the noisy city deserted; citadel and watchtower will become a wasteland forever, the delight of donkeys, a pasture for flocks, till the Spirit is poured upon us from on high, and the desert becomes a fertile field, and the fertile field seems like a forest. Justice will dwell in the desert, and righteousness live in the fertile field. The fruit of righteousness will be peace; the effect of righteousness will be quietness and confidence forever. My people will live in peaceful dwelling places, in secure homes, in undisturbed places of rest." (Isaiah 32:14-18)

The Work of the **"Spirit from on high"** in Isaiah is the renewal of Israel, rebuilding and restoring God's chosen people. It is to bring salvation's blessings and purify God's people. God's power can do so much more than our human efforts can. (Ephesians 3:20-21)

Are you clothed, or must you be clothed with this power?

Do you want to be clothed with power from on high?

Chapter 9

Keys to Being Filled with the Spirit!

I. Dependency:

Dependency is a state of relying on or being controlled by someone
or something else.

The reason Jesus said wait, or tarry, or stay was to remind the disciples
that the Great Commission was not something they could do in their
strength. The Holy Spirit is the change agent.

**"Therefore, do not be foolish but understand what the will of the
Lord is. And do not get drunk with wine, for that is debauchery, but
be filled with the Spirit."** (Ephesians 5:17)

The Holy Spirit is critical to our victorious living and our bold witness. We must always be dependent on Him!

II. Intimacy:

Intimacy generally refers to the level of proximity between two people. It means closeness, fellowship, communion, friendship, understanding, sharing, affection, familiarity, being and belonging together personally, physically, emotionally, spiritually, and mentally.

Intimacy and the infilling of the Spirit is the direct result of prayer. Acts 4:31-33 says, "And when they had prayed, the place in which they were gathered together was shaken, and they were all filled with the Holy Spirit and continued to speak the word of God with boldness. Now the full number of those who believed were of one heart and soul, and no one said that any of the things that belonged to him was his own, but they had everything in common. And with great power, the apostles were giving their testimony to the resurrection of the Lord Jesus, and great grace was upon them all."

From the above text, prayer and intimacy with the Holy Spirit produced the filling of each one with the Spirit, speaking God's word with boldness, unity among them all, a generous spirit in the people, the power to share and testify to the resurrection, and a great grace upon them all.

Luke 11:13 says, **"If you then, who are evil, know how to give good gifts to your children, how much more will the heavenly Father give the Holy Spirit to those who ask him!"**

The above text shows that God longs to give us power for the mission, but he wants us to come to him and ask. We must constantly ask God to fill us with the Holy Spirit.

III. Surrender:

Surrender means abandon, relinquish, resign, waive, and yield to another authority.

We must make ourselves available to Him. It's not about how much of the Holy Spirit you have; it's about how much the Holy Spirit has of you!

Ephesians 4:30 reads, **"And do not grieve the Holy Spirit of God..."** To grieve the Spirit is to cause the Holy Spirit to feel sadness or sorrow.

We can grieve the Spirit by our inconsistencies, corrupt and worthless conversation. (Ephesians 4:29-32)

Grieving the Holy Spirit has to do with how I speak, how I treat others, whether I am bitter or full of anger and slander someone else.

Our heavenly Father wants what is best for us.

This is why the Scripture says He is jealous over us. (Nahum 1:2).

Being born again doesn't mean we won't sin. When we sin, He expects us to come to Him in brokenness. We must not grieve the Holy Spirit. (Ephesians 4:30 NIV)

It's possible to grieve the Holy Spirit by:

1. Negative Speech. (Ephesians 4:29)

Constant complaining thrived in the camps of the Israelites in the wilderness. Nothing satisfied them. They accused Moses, doubted God's Word, and wanted to return to the land of Egypt. (Hebrews 3:7-11)

The same heartbreaking attitude can be reflected in our words if we don't keep a watch over our mouths.

2. Uncontrolled Emotions. (Ephesians 4:26, 32)

Bitterness is related to hatred. It is a root that produces bitter fruit or extreme wickedness. Wrath is indignation that can rise gradually and then subside. Anger rises when we abhor injustice.

This feeling can be used righteously, as in Jesus' temple cleansing. But we must guard ourselves against using anger in a vengeful way when we feel that we have personally been wronged. Clamor is a deep crying or wail in distress, like self-pity. Malice is the destruction of a person's character through slander or blaspheming and dis respecting God.

3. Lying. (Ephesians 4:25, 1 Corinthians 12:26)

False flattery is one way we lie to each other. We don't want to off end our brothers and sisters, but we also shouldn't say something we don't mean. What about gossip? Repeating stories and rumors about another person can harm their character and our image.

4. Falling for Deception. (Ephesians 5:6)

The troublemakers of Korah, Dathan, and Abiram came against Moses and tried to usurp his authority. (Numbers 16:1-3) In Exodus 32, the people were deceived into building a golden image.

Jesus warned about wolves in sheep's clothing coming in with false words. (Matthew 7:15).

We can only stay on course by knowing the truth and not listening to anything that contradicts the Bible.

The Holy Spirit is grieved when we believe anything other than the truth. Listening to false doctrine can draw us away from Him and into sinful actions.

5. Stealing. (Ephesians 4:28)

The size or value of an item is not what determines theft. People can steal by cheating on taxes or falsifying business documents. According to Adam Clarke's commentary, the rabbis condoned stealing if part of what was taken was given to the poor. Human nature is the same now as it was in Biblical days. God sees all and is saddened when we don't reflect His character.

6. Drunkenness. (Ephesians 5:18)

The debate about Christians drinking alcohol will probably continue until Jesus comes back. But the Scripture is clear about drunkenness. Paul had to warn the Corinthians about

drunkenness because they misused the communion table.
(2 Corinthians 11:21)

We are not to judge, but we are also told not to be a stumbling
block to another person's faith. (Rom. 14:13). We should
consider how others interpret our activities and attitudes.

A lifestyle that does not grieve the Holy Spirit must:
- Imitate of God. (Ephesians 5:1).
- Walk in love. (Ephesians 5:2).
- Be kind and forgive each other. (Ephesians 4:32)
- Purify your speech. (Ephesians 5:19).
- Give thanks. (Ephesians 5:20).
- Live in the Fruit of the Spirit; Continuing to walk in the fruit of the Spirit will keep us sensitive to His voice and empower us against temptations. If His fruit is dominant, our lives won't cause anguish to the One who lives within us. Praising the Lord will put our focus on Him instead of what our human desires demand. Rather than grieving the Spirit, we can praise and thank Him.

1 Thessalonians 5:19 says, **"Do not quench the Spirit."** *Quench* means to stifle, as in putting out a fire or a flame.

In using the word quench, Paul pictured the Spirit of God as fire (Isaiah 4:4; Acts 2:3; Revelation 4:5).

Fire speaks of purity, power, light, warmth, and, if necessary, destruction. The fire of the Spirit must not go out on the altar of our hearts. (Lev 6:12-13)

Daily, ask God to empower you by His Spirit to be bold, more attentive, and more engaged with those around you to proclaim the Good News.

Confess when you have grieved Him and His movement in your life. Ask Him to cultivate in you Dependence, Intimacy, and Surrender.

Chapter 10

Anointing/Empowerment, Gifts, and Talents

"The purpose of the oil is to keep the fire burning. It is that oil that upgrades the authority that makes you effective when you speak. It takes you to the next level and brings increase. It is the Holy Spirit anointing that makes everything that's impossible for you possible. You become unstoppable."

– Pastor Austyn

"But my horn You have exalted like a wild ox; I have been anointed with fresh oil." (Psalms 92:10)

"You anoint my head with oil; my cup runs over." (Psalm 23:5)

We must distinguish anointing with gifts and talents.

"For the gifts and the calling of God are irrevocable." (Romans 11:29)

The source of gifts, talents, and anointing is God. When God gives a gift, you can operate in it, even when the anointing is missing from your life.

Saul was king for about 13 years after the anointing had gone from him. People still function in their roles today, even after God fired them.

When you are anointed, you can tell when someone else is not anointed. It's your obedience that keeps the anointing on your life. The anointing of God takes you places your talent can't take you. Spiritual disciplines that are out of love and not legalism are the key.

Psalm 91:1,2 reads, **"He who dwells in the secret place of the Most High Shall abide under the shadow of the Almighty. I will say of the Lord, "He is my refuge and my fortress; My God, in Him I will trust."**

The above text is a call to abide constantly in the secret place. Only then can we operate in the anointing continually.

To live empowered, we must:

(1) Pray daily –1 Thessalonians 5:17 "... pray without ceasing."

(2) Spend time in God's word- Psalm 119:11: "Your word I have hidden in my heart, That I might not sin against You."

(3) Trust God- Psalm 73:28: **"But it is good for me to draw near to God;**

I have put my trust in the Lord GOD, That I may declare all Your works."

(4) Stay connected to your local church- Hebrews 10:24 says, **"And let us consider one another in order to stir up love and good works."**

The church is the only place people want to disconnect because of the things people do and say that they don't like. People do stuff you don't like on your job, yet you still go daily.

(5) Remain close to people close to God. 2 Corinthians 6:14 says, **"Do not be unequally yoked together with unbelievers. For what fellow ship has righteousness with lawlessness? And what communion has light with darkness?"** In Amos 3:3, the Scripture says, **"Can two walk together, unless they are agreed?"**

Your relationships with others can determine how close or far away you can be from God.

The anointing is the power and presence of God on and in your life.

Jesus could not have accomplished His mission without the Holy Spirit (Luke 3:22, Luke 4:14, Acts 10:38). Before He began His mission, He had to be empowered.

Christ literally means "the Anointed One".
When God's presence or affirmation is in your life, who dislikes you doesn't matter. The anointing keeps opening doors for you.
The anointing reveals things to us. (1 John 2:20)

1 Samuel 10:1: **"Then Samuel took a flask of oil and poured it on his head and kissed him and said, "Has not the Lord anointed you to be prince over his people Israel? And you shall reign over the people of the Lord, and you will save them from the hand of their surrounding enemies. And this shall be the sign to you that the Lord has anointed you to be prince over his heritage."**

Saul was anointed and became the first king of Israel. From then on, Saul was transformed and became a man of exploits.

The impact of the anointing in Saul's life:

(1) The anointing located his missing donkeys. (1Samuel 10:2)
(2) The anointing attracted resources and destiny helpers. (1 Samuel 10:2)
(3) The anointing empowered him and provoked him to act.
(4) The anointing advanced him and pushed him forward (1 Samuel 10:3)
(5) The anointing caused him to become a new man. (1 Samuel10: 7)
(6) The anointing took him from ordinary to royalty.
(7) The anointing made him a commander and leader (1 Samuel 10:1)
(8) The anointing raised him as a worshipper to God.
(9) The anointing caused people to favor his cause.
(10) The anointing connected him to people who celebrated God. (1 Samuel 10:5)
(11) The anointing enabled him to prophesy.
(12) The anointing allows us to speak God's mind with a purpose. (1 Samuel 10:6-7)

Whatever the anointing did for Saul is available to anyone who puts their faith in God.

Unfortunately, Saul became rebellious with time, and God withdrew His anointing from him. **"For rebellion is as the sin of witchcraft, And stubbornness is as iniquity and idolatry. Because you have rejected the word of the Lord, He also has rejected you from being king."** (1 Samuel 15:23)

The above text shows that Saul disqualified himself from the throne. He was rejected from being king because of his lack of brokenness whenever he sinned against God.

"But the Spirit of the Lord departed from Saul, and a distressing spirit from the Lord troubled him." (1 Samuel 16:14)

According to the scripture, we see that God has taken his hand off Saul because he had rejected the precepts of God. Saul still had his position as king, but not the hand of God on him, as it had been in the past.

Now Saul is distressed because he had a title but not the anointing. The same anointing that works through you to help others can become the source of your downfall if you do not maintain a humble heart.

We must not compromise the anointing:

Several people have compromised the anointing for immediate gain, both in Bible history and now.

Today, I met with one of the modern-day prophetic voices, who told me an unfortunate story. One of his mentors has just been exposed for sexually molesting several minors.

Unfortunately, it's said that this has been going on for some time.

"Now Jacob cooked a stew, and Esau came in from the field, and he was weary. And Esau said to Jacob, "Please feed me with that same red stew, for I am weary. Therefore his name was called Edom. But Jacob said, "Sell me your birthright as of this day." (Genesis 25:29-31)

We are the most vulnerable to attack when hungry, angry, lonely, and tired. (H.A.L.T.)

Jacob told Esau, "If you want something right now, give me your future." Esau preferred immediate gratification, which affected his whole bloodline.

Adam and Eve gave up the garden for a piece of fruit. Samson had the anointing but laid in the wrong woman's lap and got a haircut from hell. It is essential to have self-control and to maintain the posture of obedience. (1 Samuel 15:22).

Obedience is vital to receiving and maintaining the anointing. (Exodus 19:5)

Chapter 11

The Benefits of the Anointing

"Now He who establishes us with you in Christ and has anointed us is God." (2 Corinthians 1:21)

1. It's the source of your establishment. (Psalm 89:21).
2. It's the source of your Deliverance: (Psalm 89:22-23)
3. It's your source of Protection and Preservation. (Job 1:10, Daniel 3:20-26, John 11:39-44). The anointing will protect and preserve everything connected to you. (Psalm 105:14-15).
4. It's the Source of your Strength. (Judges 14:6,19,15:14). (Psalm 144:1; 18:1: 28:8;20:6,18:50; Philippians 4:14; Exodus13:21-22; 14:24-25; Judges 1:24; Colossians 2:6-7).
5. Anointing breaks the Yoke. (Isaiah 10:27).
6. The anointing will sharpen your discernment.
7. The anointing will empower you to overcome every battle. **"Your hand**

will find all your enemies: Your right hand will find those who hate You." (Psalm 21:8)

8. The anointing will protect you. (Psalm 20:6)
9. Healing: He will restore your health. And you will become a minister of His healing power.
10. Revelation: (Exodus 25:6)
11. Provision: (1 Kings 17:14)
12. Debt-free living: (2 Kings 4:1-7).
13. Deliverance. (Psalm 23:1-5)
14. Faith: In Isaiah 21:5, the watchman was directed to anoint the shield.
15. Blessings: (Psalm 133:3)
16. Guidance on the path of life. (John 16:13)
17. Strength to live righteously. (Galatians 3:13; 5:25,1 John 2:16)
18. Teaching you: (John 15:26, John 14:26).
19. Effectiveness in your prayer life. (Romans 8:26–28)
20. Uncommon comfort to you: The Holy Spirit is called the "Comforter (Counselor, Helper, Intercessor, Advocate, Strengthener, and Standby)."
21. Enablement to function in certain gifts.

HINDRANCES TO EXPERIENCING THE POWER

Several barriers keep us from experiencing God's power through the Holy Spirit.

Most barriers fall under one of four categories: sin, reliance on self, head knowledge of God's Word that does not result in heart knowledge, and failure to surrender to God's will.

"Now He could do no mighty work there, except that He laid His hands on a few sick people and healed them. And He marveled because of

their unbelief" (Mark 6:5-6).

From the above text, it appears that in Jesus' hometown, there was an atmosphere of unbelief that limited God's power.

Unbelief manifests in various ways and limits us from experiencing the fullness of the Holy Spirit's power.

1. Unbelief Disguised as "Balance."
   Some are afraid that pursuing the power of the Holy Spirit will cause them to become unbalanced. Being balanced means walking in the power of the Spirit according to Scripture's guidelines and remaining grounded in the Word.

2. An Unhealthy Fear of Deception.
   (Matthew 7:15-23). Using this logic, Moses would have refused to perform the signs that God commanded him because the Egyptian sorcerers were doing the same things. (Exodus 7:8-12)

The existence of counterfeits should not cause us to run from the real. The true power of God will always swallow up the false.

3. Putting Power Against Character.
   Nowhere in the Bible does it say that we must choose between character and power. "Pursue love, and desire spiritual gifts" (1 Corinthians 14:1). Both character and power are essential.

4. Theology that Denies Supernatural Gifts.

The Cessationist theology states that the gifts of the Holy Spirit, such as tongues, healings, miracles, and prophecy, have ceased and are no longer to be a part of the Christian experience or church life.

Some are highly skeptical of anything supernatural or attribute anything supernatural to Satan.

It is time to stop making up excuses for our unbelief. We can no longer accept powerless Christianity as normal. Let us seek a fresh outpouring of God's Spirit and a release of His power without hindrance!

5. Willful Sinning

In Genesis 2 and 3, Adam and Eve's choice to do things their way brought sin into our lives and their own. Because of Adam and Eve, we all have a sinful nature, and it affects every part of us.

"Indeed, there is no one on earth who is righteous, no one who does what is right and never sins." (Ecclesiastes 7:20)

We cannot expect to experience God's power when we willingly sin because willful sin always short-circuits the work of the Holy Spirit. It is through the confession of our sin that we are telling God that we want to have our relationship with him restored, and it is then that the Holy Spirit will empower us to do God's work under the anointing. (1 John 1:9).

6. Reliance on Self: We have an innate desire to think about ourselves first. **"For whoever finds me finds life and receives favor from the Lord."** (Proverbs 8:35)

To find favor with God and experience His power in life, we must die to self-reliance, self-trust, self-sufficiency, and independence along the pathway of life. Only when we die to ourselves will God be able to mul tiply all we are and all we have. (John 12:24–25)

7. Head Knowledge of God's Word that Does Not Result in Heart Knowl edge.
   We must study God's Word to have His power operative in our lives.

   Our knowledge must move from our head to our heart in the form of con viction that impacts our faith and behavior. Failure to do so will undoubt-edly make our lives barren and unproductive.

8. Failure to Surrender to God's Will
   A refusal to surrender to God's will is what is often referred to as being a "carnal" Christian, one who is still influenced a great deal by the world and its enticements.

   1 Corinthians 3:1 says, **"And I, brethren, could not speak unto you as unto spiritual, but as unto carnal, even as unto babes in Christ."**

   A carnal Christian has accepted the Good News of Jesus Christ but does not want to be transformed by it.

9. A Legalistic Spirit

   Satan will always want us to engage in duties of our strength. This is like putting new wine in old wineskins, and it will only lead to cycles of frustration.

In Christian theology, "legalism" refers to the idea that a person earns or merits salvation by doing good works or obeying the law.

"You foolish Galatians! Who has bewitched you? Before your very eyes Jesus Christ was clearly portrayed as crucified. I would like to learn just one thing from you: Did you receive the Spirit by the works of the law, or by believing what you heard?" (Galatians 3:1, 2)

From the above scripture, we see the possibility of focusing on our works for salvation instead of the finished work of Jesus.

The most common Signs of a Legalistic Spirit: Many people are slaves to performance-based religion.

1. Lack of true joy. Legalism kills joy. When someone encounters God's mercy, their hearts always overflow with praise and gratitude. (Romans 14:17).

2. No real victory over sin. All Christians face temptations. But a person with a legalistic mindset finds it challenging to receive the grace of God to overcome sinful habits.

3. Unhealthy performance orientation. Many people feel they must earn His love by reading the Bible, praying, giving, and performing other religious tasks.

4. A critical, unloving attitude toward others. People who don't understand God's grace cannot extend grace to anyone else. Some Christians are still hateful toward unbelievers and even fellow believers. When you hear Christians using harsh language to condemn others; you have just identified a legalistic spirit.

5. Obsessive focus on outward standards of dress or behavior. Some Christians have condemned makeup, jewelry, pants, and short hair for women. Others taught that it was wrong for Christians to play sports, play cards, dance, wear wedding rings, go to movies, wear jeans in church, or even own a television! God emphasizes inner holiness rather than outward conformity. When you walk in grace, the Spirit will lead you to dress and act in a way that honors Him.

6. Bondage to religious tradition. A legalistic spirit says, "This is how we've always done it." Some people rejected a new move of the Holy Spirit because they didn't like a new style of music.

7. A sectarian attitude toward other Christians. Some churches teach that they are the only people going to heaven.

8. Little or no assurance of salvation. A genuine encounter with Jesus will cause you to know that God has adopted you and will never abandon you. (Romans 8:15). A genuine encounter with God will lead to a life-long transformation process. (Romans 12:1-3)

9. Unspiritual company. A company of carnal, unregenerate people and graceless, nominal professing Christians will be a hindrance. (1 Corinthians 15:33, Hebrews 3:13).

10. Careless talk. Your heart can be turned out of frame by loud, violent, hasty, and much talk, even in good things. (Proverbs 14:23; James 3:5-6; Proverbs 17:27; Matthew 15:8)

11. Overindulging. Excess in using food, drink, and other recreations can be the ordinary inlet of many evils. (Luke 21:34; Proverbs 25:27

and 23:20-21).

12. Carelessness about devotions. Omitting private duties or carelessly doing them. This includes duties such as prayer, self-examination, meditation, and reading (Matthew 26:41; Proverbs 23:21).

13. Neglecting spontaneous silent prayer. Neglecting spontaneous silent prayer when conversing with others. (Matthew 26:41).

14. Vain thoughts (Jeremiah 4:14).

15. Not keeping the heart. (Matthew 26:41). It's possible to lose in public what you gained in private!

16. Discouragements and unbelief. These will arise from feelings of what I lack, sins, and trials. These will weaken your hands. (1 Samuel 12:20; Lamentations 1:9; Jeremiah 2:28;Hebrews 12:12-13). It was when Peter started to be afraid that he began to sink.

17. Being too absorbed in temporal things. These will distract you and make you utterly unable to serve God (Luke 10:4 and 21:34).

18. Pride. Pride and thinking much of yourself, self-boasting, seeking the praise of men, and seeking to exalt yourself by being careless in duties. (Romans 9:31-32).

19. Slothfulness. Slothfulness in sleeping too long and trifling away time will "cloth anyone with rags".

Chapter 12

Ingredients/Principles for Keeping Your Anointing

"But my horn shalt thou exalt like the horn of an unicorn: I shall be anointed with fresh oil." (Psalm 92:10)

According to Exodus 30:22-25, the sacred anointing oil was made of five ingredients: MYRRH, CINNAMON, CALAMUS, CASSIA, AND A HIN OF OLIVE OIL

This anointing oil was used for kings and priests and to consecrate those things meant to be most holy. These five ingredients can be considered some of the principles of living an effective, anointed life—a life God can use to accomplish His will and purposes.

(1) The first ingredient of an anointed life is meekness and submission to God's will.

The first ingredient was a spice called **myrrh**.'

Myrrh is a fragrance from the trunk of a Commiphora tree in Arabia. It's produced in the form of tears. Alcohol is added to remove any impurities, and then the gum is steamed. As the steam passes through the gum, it melts into oil, which becomes a perfume.

Meekness is not a weakness. It's submitting all that you have in obedience to God; when you do that, the anointing attracts your life.

Numbers 12:3 says that Moses was the meekest man who ever lived. It took Moses 40 years to come to this level of meekness. He put his self-will and said yes to God despite himself.

(2) The second ingredient of an anointed life is uprightness, or how you stand. The second ingredient in the anointing oil was **cinnamon**.

Cinnamon comes from a tree that grows 30 to 40 feet, grows remarkably straight, and has no curves. They squeeze the leaves and fruit of that upright tree, and out of that comes the oil. They used cinnamon oil to make fragrant candles for the king.

Integrity matters. Being upright means standing for what is right, standing on the truth, living above reproach, and not judging those around you.

Today, when we speak of ill-doing people, we call them "crooked."

(3) The third ingredient of an anointed life is humility. The recipe for God's holy anointing included *calamus*, a reed that grows in swamps.

The head of the reed is filled with oil. You know it's ready to be used when the head of the reed is bent over, almost in half. It speaks of bending low in humility.

Jesus demonstrated this level of humility. When asked, **"Who shall be greatest in your kingdom?" He said he is the one who is willing to serve others."**

In an ultimate act of humility, the hands that created the universe washed the disciple's feet. This was His example of how to be great.

(4) The fourth ingredient for an anointed life is cleansing.

Malachi 3:2 says, **"He [The Lord] is like a refiner's fire, and like fullers' soap."**

The fourth ingredient in the anointing oil was called *cassia*. *Cassia* produces a leaf called senna that, still today, is used for inner cleansing.

The Holy Spirit comes to clean us, like a refiner's fire burning off the scum, turning up the heat until only the purest substance remains. And like fullers' soap, the outside is washed clean once the inside is purified.

Everything must be brought to the cross, laid at the altar, and you need to say,

"Search me, O God, and know my heart: try me, and know my thoughts:

And see if there be any wicked way in me and lead me in the way everlasting." (Psalm 139: 23-24).

Are you letting things into your life that are hindering the anointing?

(5) The fifth ingredient to an anointed life is the Holy Spirit, the presence of God in your life.

A hin, or container of olive oil, was the final ingredient required to make the sacred ointment. Olive oil symbolizes the Holy Spirit.

Olive oil was used to cook food in ancient days, to bring rest and comfort by applying it to their feet after a long journey, to pour on wounds to bring healing, and to anoint kings, priests, and prophets. Today, the Holy Spirit, who came to us after Christ ascended into Heaven, brings comfort, power, and healing and fills us so that we never hunger or thirst again.

There's nothing worse than old, stale oil; it attracts flies, and Satan is Beelzebub, the Lord of the Flies.

Fighting today's battles, depending on yesterday's oil, is futile. It would be best if you had the daily presence of the Holy Spirit in your life. You need an ongoing relationship through worship, prayer, and the Word. You cannot sustain an anointed life on a stale, forgotten relationship with God. It would be best if you had a fresh anointing. (Psalm 92:10)

Material things cannot substitute for God's fresh move in your life. You must stay sensitive to the guidance of the Holy Spirit. We must not operate in the spirit of pride.

Pride will have you excuse or blame others for your faults, but humility will make you admit your faults. (Psalm 51:11)

Anointed people are humble, just like Jesus was.

It would help if you refused to let fear drive your decisions. (1 Samuel 15:24)

We need to do what God wants us to and not be concerned with what people will think of us.

When walking in the anointing, know that God has his hand on you, even when people reject you.

God's promises to the anointed:
(Memorize and meditate on the scriptures daily.)

"Now I know that the Lord saves His anointed; He will answer him from His holy heaven with the saving strength of His right hand." (Psalm 20:6)

"Do not touch My anointed ones And do My prophets no harm." (1 Chronicles 16:22)

"You love righteousness and hate wickedness; Therefore God, Your God, has anointed You With the oil of gladness more than Your companions." (Psalm 45:7)

"God will save his anointed because He keeps you as the apple of His eyes and has written your name in the palms of His hands." (Psalm 17:8)

Chapter 13

Stewardship Determines Your Value Here and In Eternity!

(THE MEASURE OF A LIFE)?

The measure of a man is not how much he has but how much he gives for God's glory.

How we handle what we have, including our lives, is called stewardship.

In the ancient world, stewardship was not a religious term but was a key component of commerce. Almost every business concern had a steward who served like an ancient chief operating officer, running the daily affairs of the house's master.

A steward was someone entrusted with the management of someone else's affairs.

In the Bible, any leadership is stewardship.

This can be leading a country, business, church committee, community organization, family, or yourselves. Paul's exhortation to Timothy on leadership selection for the early church applies to leaders in all these areas. (1 Timothy 3:1-7)

Peter Block defines stewardship as the willingness to be held accountable for the well-being of the larger organization by operating in service, rather than control, of those around us.

Money is a tiny part of our stewardship.

Stewardship is about how we live our lives.

Stewardship is the management of your life for God. How do you measure the success of your stewardship?

Is your life a reflection of good stewardship? How do we establish godly values and ensure we will be good stewards?

Building a godly value system:

"By faith Moses, when he had grown up, refused to be known as the son of Pharaoh's daughter. He chose to be mistreated along with the people of God rather than to enjoy the fleeting pleasures of sin. He regarded disgrace for the sake of Christ as of greater value than the treasures

of Egypt, because he was looking ahead to his reward. By faith he left Egypt, not fearing the king's anger; he persevered because he saw him who is invisible. By faith he kept the Passover and the application of blood, so that the destroyer of the firstborn would not touch the first-born of Israel." (Hebrews 11:24-28)

From the above verses, we can learn from the life of Moses:

1. Relationship with God is a treasure far better than this world and this life.
2. God is to be feared above earthly kings.
3. Obedience to God's instruction is ultimately for His glory and our good.

   - Faith will rearrange our value system. (Vs 27.) All of life must rest upon a foundation of confidence in God and His Word.

   - Values must be based on Faith (Vs. 25-26). The will and purpose of God must be given greater value than the things of this life.

   - Choices must be based upon values (Vs. 24-25)

Had we been there, we might have tried to talk Moses out of it, but he made the right decisions. Eternity rejoices over his life. So do we.

A moment came when Moses began calculating life differently. He considered Christ's shame or disgrace **"greater wealth"** than all the **"treasures of Egypt."**

In all this, Moses **"was looking to the reward."** And the reward is precisely what he received.

First, he participated in God's workings on earth. Secondly, he received an incredible legacy; he became God's instrument. Thirdly, he gained eternity with God. Fourthly, he entered a friendship with God. Fifthly, he overcame Egypt's oppression through the power of God.

Measuring the Success of Our Stewardship

A. The esteem of others does not measure success. (Luke 12:1-2)

The word "hypocrite" originated from Greek theater. It means to "wear a mask," to play a role, to be false. It refers to hiding one's real motives and character behind a mask of sincerity.

The religious hypocrite plays his role to convince others that he is something more than he is.

It is pretended devotion. It is premeditated deception.

The folly of hypocrisy is that the mask will eventually come off. We may be successful at deceiving others, but we never deceive God.

Whether through the circumstances of life or at His seat of justice, God will expose the true nature of the hypocrite. What others esteem you to be is not important, but what God knows you to be.

B. Our possessions do not measure success. (Luke 12:14-21)

Covetousness is a craving for something we think will make life more satisfying. It's when the heart desperately reaches out for something God has denied for the present.

Covetousness comes from the belief that having more makes life more satisfying and the person more valuable. Possessions are only for a time, but your soul is eternal.

Success is not measured by what you have now but by what endures for eternity.

C. *The things we need are different from the measure of our Success.* *(Luke 12:22-30)*

Worry is the mental distress caused by uncertainty. Anxiety arises from a lack of faith in God's promises and dependence upon God's provision. Security is not found in the substance of life but in the Source of life.

D. *The success of a life is measured by its relationship to eternity.* *(Luke 12: 31-40)*

The priority of a hypocrite is appearances.

The priority of the covetous person is possessions.

The priority of the anxious person is security.

The priority of a faithful steward is eternity.

Jesus said, **"What shall it profit a man, if he shall gain the whole world, and lose his soul."**

Matthew 25 reminds us that our money, health, time, and skills are unrelated to our spiritual life. The way we view our resources is related to our spiritual lives.

This chapter calls us to deeper faith and trust in Jesus Christ.

God does not always reward faith with material blessings, and we are called to live by faith, not sight. Biblically, we know that poverty, blessings, or bad health are not always linked to a person's righteousness.

Jesus lived a perfect, sinless life and gave it willingly in the place of sinners as a substitute. He bore the wrath of us and freely gave us his righteousness. He died, and three days later, He rose from the dead by the power of God. And to those who trust in Him, He gives eternal life and the indwelling of the Holy Spirit.

Our finances, talents, time, and health are all areas where we have opportunities to glorify God, who saved us.

Colossians 3:17 says, **"And whatever you do, in word or deed, do everything in the name of the Lord Jesus, giving thanks to God the Father through him."**

The question is always how we can do **"everything in the name of the Lord Jesus."**

From the parable of talents, God the master owns everything and does not owe anyone anything.

Job 41:11 says, **"Who has first given to me, that I should repay him? Whatever is under the whole heaven is mine."**

The secret to managing God's gifts is not running from them but understanding why He has given them to us in the first place.

- **God gives people their wealth.**

1 Corinthians 4:7 – **"For who sees anything different in you? What do you have that you did not receive? If then you received it, why do you boast as if you did not receive it?"**

The famous King David of Israel recognized the truth of the above scripture. To help build the temple, the Israelites gave things they owned. But David's prayer in response was: **"O Lord our God, all this abundance that we have provided for building you a house for your holy name comes from your hand and is all your own."** (1 Chronicles 29:16)

The most essential thing in life is how we steward what God has given us.

(1) We don't own what we have.
Think of someone who goes into a supermarket. Walking through the aisles, he takes goods from the shelves and puts them under his arms. As he goes out without paying for the goods, they confront him with, "What are you taking those items, sir?" Then he replies, "These goods are mine. I collected them and have them under my arm." If you were the store owner, what would be your response?

No wonder God speaks about people robbing him. (Malachi 3:9-10)

What we have in our possession is not truly ours. You came into the world with nothing and will leave with nothing.

(2) We're only stewards of what we've been given.

Stewardship changes our view of our bank accounts, vehicles, homes, and other possessions in 4 main ways:

1. They're not to be used for our sole purpose but God's.
2. We'll be held accountable for using our master's wealth. (Romans 14:12)
3. We must justify how we use all our wealth, not just what we give to church and others, but what we also spend on ourselves.
4. Getting wealthy isn't an end in itself.

Are you a poor steward or a good steward?

- **Poor Stewardship is Evidence of No Faith**

In the parable of talents in Mathew 25, the unfaithful servant is called lazy and wicked. He did not lose it, but he did not increase it. He neglected his responsibility and didn't consider his master worthy. The consequence of this was to be thrown into darkness – into hell.

- **God is very serious about stewardship.**

The faithful servants did not know when the master would return, but they trusted that he would, so they went out, worked hard, and increased what they were given. The unfaithful servant decided to play it safe and not risk. Now, either he thought the master wouldn't return as promised or that faithfulness would not be rewarded when he did return. The unfaithful servant decided to bury the talent and spend his time doing something else.

Misusing God what God has entrusted to us is the same as stealing from God. We find out about this in the book of Malachi.

The good servants trusted the master's word and goodness. The unfaithful servant had faith in neither the master's word nor his goodness.

If you're living solely for yourself and the increase of wealth, with no desire to serve God, then it's pretty likely that you do not have faith in God.

This parable is also about the difference between heaven and hell. Do you have faith, and what's your destination?

- **We glorify God when we choose to be faithful stewards**.

The first two servants were called good and faithful because they were immediately obedient and productive, took risks, were patient enough to wait until the Master returned, and finally received profitable returns. God didn't only tell us what to do with the resources we have, but in His love, He showed us how.

Love for God should be our number one motivation to be good stewards. Love for God marks someone who Christ has forgiven.

That love for God will include a desire to use our resources to please Him.

1 Peter 4:10 says, **"As each has received a gift, use it to serve one another, as good stewards of God's varied grace."**

The second motive for being a faithful steward is Christ's return.

In the parable, the Master returned to settle accounts.

2 Corinthians 5:10 says, **"For we must all appear before the judgment**

seat of Christ, so that each one may receive what is due for what he has done in the body, whether good or evil."

What we do while on earth has implications for gaining or losing rewards in heaven. We should expect every day to be the day Christ will return, which must be reflected in our decisions. Will you be found faithful, and are you ready to account for what you have done with what He has entrusted you with?

Good stewardship will free us from being overwhelmed by lousy life circumstances and from guilt while allowing us to enjoy what God has given to us.

The decision to live a life of generosity will glorify God. It's not about amounts and appearances but whether your heart is fully surrendered to Jesus first.

To be a good steward, you must:
    a. Acknowledgement of God's ownership. (Deuteronomy 8:18)
    b. Recognition of God's gifts. (1 Peter 4:10)
    c. Be understanding and committed. (Proverbs 16:3. 1; Thessalonians 2:4)
    d. Be trustworthy. (Proverbs 12:22, Titus 1:7)
    e. Be diligent. (1 Corinthians 15:38. Proverbs 13:4)
    f. Be prayerful. (James 1:5, Philippians 4:6)
    g. Be action-oriented. (1 Peter 1:13)

Chapter 14

The M's of Successful Stewardship

Practicing good stewardship is a way of life. We must believe that God is the source of every "good and perfect gift" and that we are accountable to Him for all He gives us.

Stewardship is the faithful, careful, and responsible management of everything and everyone God entrusts to our care.

Cultivating stewardship does not begin with our relationship with God but extends to others. Successful stewardship is the principled, multidimensional development of our life in Christ, our families, the Church, and our "neighbors."

The Messenger. No one can be an effective messenger without having a personal relationship with the sender. Moses first encountered God before he was given a message to proclaim to his generation.

The Message. Successful stewardship starts with a clear and compelling message of repentance. (Matthew 3:2) This is the change of your mind and way of living if you want to enter the Kingdom of God.

Jesus' first message at the onset of His public ministry should be our central message.

The Mission. Jesus told His disciples: **"Go and make disciples of all nations, baptizing them in the name of the Father and of the Son and of the Holy Spirit."** (Matthew 28:19)

His "Great Commission" is our great co-mission.

Dedicated believers are not passive spectators but goers.

The Ministry. The Greek word for ministry is service. All excellent customer service leads to more sales. While the Church is not a business, the Lord Himself is the ultimate example of outstanding service. (Matthew 20:28).

This will include educational programs, pastoral care, prayer, fellowship, hospitality, mission, etc.

The Meaning. The disciples **"left everything"** (Luke 5:11), their livelihoods, their homes, their families, etc., to follow Him.

They had found what gave meaning to their lives. We are likewise called to carry our cross daily and follow Him.

The Money. God commands us to be fruitful, which applies to our finances. We must be diligent and apply godly wisdom for multiple sources of income.

Like other disciplines such as prayer, fasting, and reading the word, stewardship money well is essential for cultivating spiritual growth. Jesus' first commandment is to love God with all one's heart, soul, strength, and mind. Loving Him with all of one's strength and mind includes generously giving one's time, talents, and treasure.

"The first of the first fruits of your ground you shall bring into the house of the Lord your God." (Exodus 23:19).

Tithing refers to God's command to give the first 10% of one's income towards advancing His purposes on earth.

The degree to which God expects the faithful to adhere to this principle is made clear when He accuses those who don't do so of robbing Him.

"Will a man rob God? Yet you are robbing me. But you say, 'How are we robbing thee?' In your tithes and offerings... Bring the full tithes into the storehouse, that there may be food in my house; and thereby put me to the test, says the Lord of hosts, if I will not open the windows of heaven for you and pour down for you an overflowing blessing." (Malachi 3: 8-10)

Some point out that tithing is emphasized more in the Old Testament than in the New Testament. While this is technically correct, they need to notice that the principles of first fruit-giving and tithing are not diminished by the coming of Jesus Christ.

They are expanded and enhanced by His life and teachings. Jesus' disciples **"left everything and followed him"** (Luke 5:11.).

Jesus told the man seeking eternal life: **"If you would be perfect, go, sell what you possess and give to the poor, and you will have treasure in heaven; and come, follow me."** (Matthew 19:21)

The most essential method of cultivating successful stewardship is total commitment.

The Miracles. One miracle is worth more than 1000 eloquent sermons without power. Jesus' ministry was both in words and deeds. He called the disciples and gave them the power to heal and cast out demons, and they did. The early church had unusual miracles, and there is no way we would have been influential in the Kingdom without miracles.

A way of life that has God and His Kingdom as its top priority and lovingly applies the 7 M's, will be a life of impact.

Successful development begins with developing something or someone ....

Who or what is your organization developing, and why?

How well is it doing that? Is it a good and trustworthy steward of its current resources?

What is your organization's clear and compelling case for support?

When you're clear about all those things, work on developing good relationships with your donors and constituents before asking them for money…. If you do all these things well, you will be pleasantly surprised by (A) how natural it feels to ask people for gifts and (B) how generously people will give in return.

"Every faculty you have, your power of thinking or of moving your limbs from moment to moment, is given you by God. If you devoted every moment of your whole life exclusively to His service, you could not give Him anything that was not in a sense His own already." – C. S. Lewis

"What does stewardship look like in our lives today?

I believe that stewardship is where the concepts of LIFE, FAITH, WORK and ECONOMICS intersect.

Faithful people are active stewards, and this takes work.

The foundation of stewardship is faithfulness and trustworthiness.

"Now it is required that those who have been given a trust must prove faithful." (1 Corinthians 4:2)

Stewardship is "God-given responsibility with accountability!"

The following are fundamental principles of stewardship that we must understand and practice:

1. Ownership. (Psalm 24:1, 1 Corinthians 6:20)

   "You belong to God, and He owns everything." (James 1:17)

"Everything comes from you, and we have given you only what comes from your hand." (1 Chronicles 29:14)

"Everything under heaven belongs to me." (Job 41:11b)

Stewardship is the commitment of oneself and possessions to God's services.

"Remember the LORD your God, for it is he who gives you the ability to produce wealth." (Deuteronomy 8:17-18)

2. Responsibility: God has graciously entrusted us with the care, development, and Enjoyment of everything he owns. As his stewards, we are responsible for managing his holdings well and according to his desires and purposes.

3. Accountability: Like the servants in the Parable of the Talents in Matthew 25, we will be called to give an account of how we have administered everything we have been given. This includes time, money, abilities, information, wisdom, relationships, and authority.

4. You can decrease or increase what God has given you. (Matthew 25:16-18)

Evaluate Your Rate of Increase Based on What Was Given to You, Not Someone Else.

This parable leads to self-evaluation, but we can't compare ourselves to someone else and decide how well we're doing. (2 Corinthians 10: 12)

5. Live With a Sense of Urgency.
   Note the word immediately. (16-17)
   "The good servants felt the responsibility of their assignment and went to work without delay."

6. God can call you into account at any time; it may be today —
   (Matthew 25:19 – 30)

   A. He will reward the faithful: Three rewards are given here: *praise-filled approval, greater responsibility* and *eternal joy.*

   B. He will judge the faithless: The third servant made excuses for his lack of service, and he is called wicked (worthless) and lazy. Three-fold judgment: Receives no praise, No further work or responsibility, and no joy in the master's presence.
      • *Wicked means Actively evil; it's a word used by Satan.*
      • *Lazy means the type that never does anything but manages to create trouble.*

      Good stewardship of the little things leads to more extraordinary privilege and responsibility. Poor stewardship leads to losing what you have.

   C. Be ready; it could happen today. (Matthew 25:19)
      The servants had no idea when their master would return. Just like in the parable of the ten virgins. Jesus calls all this to be ready. (Matthew 24:42,44, 25: 13)

      Are you ready for His coming? Remember that His coming will also be a day of accountability, reward, or retribution.

7. Reward. (Col 3:23-24): Faithful stewards who do the master's will, with the master's resources, can expect to be rewarded in this life but entirely in the next. (Matthew 25:21)

Stewardship connects everything we do with what God is doing in the world.

8. Humility and Trust. (Proverbs 3:5-6)
   Approach stewardship with a humble heart, recognizing our dependence on God.
   - Humility extends to relationships with others. (Philippians 2:3)
   - Humility challenges us to prioritize the needs of others, promoting unity and cooperation in our personal and community lives.

9. Diligence. (1 Peter 4:10, 2 Timothy 2:15): **"Lazy hands make for poverty, but diligent Hands bring wealth."** (Proverbs 4:10)

Stewards recognize that diligence is a means of honoring God and con tributing to the well-being of others.

10. Multiplication. (Genesis 1:28a, Galatians 6:7-9)

Healthy things typically grow and reproduce. The growth we see is often based on how much we are willing to give of our time, spiritual gifts, and other resources.

11. Planning. (Proverbs 21:5, Jeremiah 29:11)

Strategic planning is a crucial aspect of responsible stewardship. We need to set goals, make informed decisions, and consider the l ong-term consequences of our actions.

12. Sacrifice. (Mark 8:34, Ephesians 5:25): The Bible is full of stories, illustrations, and parables regarding giving up something valuable for a higher purpose.

13. Generosity. (2 Cor 9:6-7): Stewardship is a heart issue that asks us to share what we God has given us resources to share with others, such as time, energy, money, and love.

    Good stewardship requires the risk of faith, commitment to excellence, and hard work.

    Good stewards are not only ready but eagerly wait for the return of their masters.

    If the master warned you of His coming for you in the next five minutes, can you say you are ready? If not, you can be prepared by asking Him to forgive your sins.

About the Author

Pastor Fred Kasule is the founder of *Go International Foundation Uganda* as well as the Overseer of *Cornerstone Christian Fellowship* churches in Uganda. He holds a Bachelor's degree in Economics and Statistics from Makerere University and is also a graduate of the International Bible Institute of London.

A Bible teacher, author and preacher, Pastor Fred holds regular crusades and conferences in Uganda and abroad.

He is married to Robina, and they have three daughters: Phillipa, Christine and Tracy Dianne.

Pastor Fred is the author of life-changing books including:
Your Dream-A great challenge, Your Dream-The Power to Become, Grace for the Race, You are God's Battle Axe and *Built to Last.*

For more information you can contact us on: +256(0)758 187 771 (WhatsApp) +256(0)772 502 853
Email: fredkasule@mail.com   **Website:** www.gifuganda.org

www.ingramcontent.com/pod-product-compliance
Lightning Source LLC
Chambersburg PA
CBHW071016120626
46546CB00003B/1106